Front Cover On 22nd August 2009, a rare perfect summers day, 44806 restarts the 2pm ex-Llangollen from the picturesque station at Berwyn.

Midcheshireman

Back Cover 7822 FOXCOTE MANOR approaches Berwyn Tunnel with the third train of the day on 1st October 2020.

Nathan Wilson

Above 5199 couldn't look much better running towards Carrog with the Suburbans during the Llangollen Railway's Along Southern Lines event on 15th October 2017.

Lawrie Rose

Published by Mainline & Maritime Ltd, 3 Broadleaze, Upper Seagry, near Chippenham, SN15 5EY
Tel: 07770 748615
www.mainlineandmaritime.co.uk orders@mainlineandmaritime.co.uk
Printed in the UK

ISBN: 978-1-900340-91-5

Great Western 0-4-2T 1450 and 0-6-0PT 9466 attract a crowd at the east end of Llangollen station.

Midcheshireman

14xx 1450 powering through Berwyn with a goods train bound for Carrog during the *Steel, Steam and Stars IV* event on 13th March 2015.
Kenny Felstead

1450 is seen in an auto sandwich near fisherman's crossing during *Steel, Steam and Stars IV* on the 7th of March 2015.

Martyn Tattam

Ex GWR 0-6-0PT 1501 running as a light engine and providing an *Evening Rambler* driver experience course, seen at Glyndyfrdwy on 1st August 2017.

Leslie Platt

The fourth *Steel, Steam and Stars* event at the Llangollen Railway saw 4270 visiting from the Gloucestershire Warwickshire Railway for the event. She is seen here with the demonstration freight at the 1000 yard straight in perfect sunny conditions on the 7th of March 2015.

Martyn Tattam

Churchward 2-8-0T 5224 leaves Llangollen with *Y Ddraig Cymraeg* (*The Welsh Dragon*).

Midcheshireman

Recreating a common combination that was found on the *Cambrian Coast Express*, visiting loco 4566 is seen double heading with 7822 FOXCOTE MANOR having just come off the 1000 yard straight on the 10th of April 2016.

Martyn Tattam

On May 17th 1992 visiting 4566 fails to disturb the sheep whilst heading the 16.50 Glyndyfrdwy to Llangollen.

Simon Fosbury

Ex-GWR Small Prairie No 4566 (from the Severn Valley Railway) departing from Berwyn during the *Along Cambrian Lines* Steam Gala on 9th April 2016.

Jeff Albiston

Former Great Western small prairie 4575 class No. 5526 works out of Llangollen and past Goods Junction in late afternoon sunshine with a solo autocoach in tow. 19th April 2009.

Phil Jones

GWR 2-6-2T 5541 nears Glyndyfrdwy in June 1996.

Dave Collier

Prairie Tank 5199 with the 1pm from Llangollen *Mince Pie Special* at Garth y Dwr on 28th December 2017.

Ben Collier

A view of the River Dee and Llangollen station taken in spring - prairie tank 5199 is is process of running around its train.

Midcheshireman

Two Great Western tank locomotives at Llangollen. 0-6-2T 5643 comes off shed, whilst 2-6-2T 5199 passes with a demonstration freight, seen at *Steel, Steam and Stars I*.

Midcheshireman

5643 near Glyndyfrdwy on 19th April 2009.

Dave Collier

6430 crosses the River Dee with an auto train.

Midcheshireman

In this 2006 view, the original chain bridge over the River Dee forms the foreground as pannier 6430 waits at Berwyn with an auto train - in more recent times the chain bridge has been dismantled and fully rebuilt.

Midcheshireman

6430 with the auto coaches at Ty Newydd on 14th May 2016.

Jeff Albiston

Auto-Fitted Pannier 6430 with the Auto-Train passes Garth y Dwr Farm on 15th October 2017.

James Kindred

Severn Valley Railway based GWR Pannier Tank 7714 heads away from Carrog along the Corwen extension during the *Along Cambrian Lines 2* event on 14th October 2018.

Kenny Felstead

Resident ex GWR pannier tank 7754 arrives at Carrog in June 1997.

Dave Collier

7754 after arriving at Llangollen station in June 2003.

Leslie Platt

This October 1989 view shows pannier tank 7760, visiting from the Birmingham Railway Museum, awaiting its next turn of duty on shed at Llangollen.

Dave Collier

Didcot Railway Centre based ex-GWR railmotor No. 93, rests with its trailer at Carrog, prior to returning to Llangollen.

Midcheshireman

Newly repainted into black for the wonderful *Steel, Steam and Stars* Galas, Dukedog No.9017 leads a photocharter goods train into Carrog during a stunning spring evening on 1st April 2009.

Phil Jones

Looking at home on Welsh territory Collett Goods 3205 is seen coming off the curve onto the 1000 yard straight with a matching rake of MK1 Suburban coaching stock during Steam, Steel and Stars IV on the 7th of March 2015.

Martyn Tattam

The classic Great Western combination of CITY OF TRURO and Dukedog 9017 leaving Glyndyfrdwy during the 2009 *Steel, Steam and Stars* event..

Midcheshireman

3440 CITY OF TRURO heads a demonstration freight near Glyndyfrdwy on 19th April 2009.

Dave Collier

3802 at Garth y Dwr in the autumn sunshine during the *Along Branch Lines* Steam Gala on 11th September 2015.

Jeff Albiston

6960 RAVENINGHAM HALL with *The Zulu*.

Midcheshireman

Visiting from the Severn Valley Railway, Manor class No.7812 ERLESTOKE MANOR leads long time resident Manor No.7822 FOXCOTE MANOR out of the mist and off 1000 yard straight near Garth y Dwr with a photographic charter. 3rd September 2013.

Phil Jones

Manor Class 7820 DINMORE MANOR (visiting from the Gloucestershire-Warwickshire Railway) with 7822 FOXCOTE MANOR at Garth y Dwr during the *Along Cambrian Lines* Steam Gala on 9th April 2016.

Jeff Albiston

The first pairing of Black Manors since the 1950s? Manor No. 7820 DINMORE MANOR pilots 7822 FOXCOTE MANOR through Carrog station during another stunning recreation of times gone by with a photocharter. 13th April 2016.

Phil Jones

4-6-0 7822 FOXCOTE MANOR approaches Pentrefelin Crossing with a *Santa Special* during the 1990s.

Midcheshireman

Manor 7822 FOXCOTE MANOR heads away from Carrog with a Corwen bound service during the *Along Birkenhead Lines* Gala on 4th March 2017.

Kenny Felstead

7822 FOXCOTE MANOR runs round its train at Carrog on 10th Septermber 2020.

Mark Faulkner

The tender of 7822 FOXCOTE MANOR is loaded with coal in anticipation of a forthcoming Steam Gala on 8th-10th April 2006.

Leslie Platt

7828 ODNEY MANOR departs from Berwyn in June 1990.

Dave Collier

Rebuilt West Country class Pacific 34027 TAW VALLEY, disguised as long-scrapped classmate 34045 OTTERY ST MARY, prepares to leave Llangollen during a 1980s Gala Weekend.

Midcheshireman

Visiting Bulleid 34053 SIR KEITH PARK climbs under the road bridge shortly after leaving Berwyn station on 15th October 2017.
James Kindred

Unrebuilt Bulleid pacific 34081 92 SQUADRON pulls away from Goods Junction Llangollen with empty stock.

Midcheshireman

The unusual Combination of a West Country Pacific and a GWR 2-8-0 as 34092 CITY OF WELLS and 3802 are seen heading towards Fisherman's with a Demonstration Freight Train during *Steel, Steam and Stars IV* on the 7th of March 2015.

Martyn Tattum

An unusual combination of veteran tank engines drifts down from Garth y Dwr and approach Ty Newydd with a demonstration freight in the 1990s. The locomotives are LNWR coal tank 1054 (leading) and Midland half cab 41708.

Midcheshireman

The weather seemed determined to try and spoil the *Steel, Steam and Stars III* event. Downpours were frequent and sunshine at a premium - at least there was plenty of steam as demonstrated by the coal tank 1054 and 828, the Caley 0-6-0, as they depart from Berwyn.

Midcheshireman

Jinty 47298 shunting a train of military vehicles at Carrog on 4th August 1996.

Midcheshireman

The 10:00 From Llangollen to Carrog reaches Glyndyfrdwy, headed by the Caledonian Railway 828 and Black Five 44806 masquerading as 44801 with Scottish links, during *Steel, Steam and Stars III* on 23rd April 2012.

Leslie Platt

Having obtained a clear road from the Glyndyfrdwy signalman, the pick-up goods is ready to depart behind LMS 0-6-0 No. 12322, the driver blows the whistle to get the fireman and pilotman back onto the footplate. The building behind the train has an interesting history - it was once the foreman's office and signing on point at Northwich shed, 8E, in Cheshire. When 8E finally closed it was dismantled and reassembled here. It is therefore the last surviving part of 8E, the rest is now demolished and a housing estate occupies the site.

Midcheshireman

LNWR Super D 49395 doing the job it was built for - moving freight. The location is just west of Berwyn.

Midcheshireman

An elevated view of Stanier mogul 42968 in action - note the almost empty tender and the tea can over the firehole door.

Midcheshireman

Visiting from the Great Central Railway, Ivatt 2 46521 departs Berwyn during the *Along Cambrian Lines 2* Gala on 14th October 2018.

Kenny Felstead

Two views of 6100 ROYAL SCOT leaving Llangollen on 19th April 2009.

Both: Dave Collier

An autumn scene at Berwyn from 2008 - 4F 0-6-0 44422 hurries a non stop local freight through the station.

Midcheshireman

Ex-LMS 8F No 48624 (visiting from the Great Central Railway) at Garth-Y-Dwr with a freight train during the *Along Birkenhead Lines* Steam Gala on 4th March 2017.

Jeff Albiston

An easy task for Stanier class 5 4-6-0 44806 as it plods past Garth y Dwr with a lightweight demonstration freight.

Midcheshireman

The 13.00 from Llangollen arrives at Berwyn behind 44806 on 18th January 2009.

Leslie Platt

45337, masquerading as scrapped classmate 45292, at Ty Newydd with a demonstration freight train during the *Along Birkenhead Lines* Steam Gala on 4th March 2017.

Jeff Albiston

Now moved onto the East Lancashire Railway, Black Five 45337, running as long lost sister 45292 heads a mixed goods towards Berwyn Tunnel on the same occasion.

Kenny Felstead

Black 5 45337 is seen masquerading as 44680 with a demo freight at Garth y Dwr on a wet and cold 5th March 2017.

Martyn Tattam

Glyndyfrdwy station sees ex Great Eastern N7 0-6-2 69621 with a suburban train bound ostensibly for Liverpool Street cross Great Western pannier tank 6430 with a typical ex GW auto train.

Midcheshireman

Rush hour at Llangollen Goods Junction. Great Northern Railway N2 1744 waits on the shed exit road, behind it is the Super D at the head of the demonstration freight and behind that the coal tank on the passenger service waiting impatiently for the Goods Junction starter signal to clear. At the start of a big gala this is a very busy place!

Midcheshireman

Visiting from the North Yorkshire Moors Railway, ex North Eastern Railway 2392 makes light work of the 1 in 80 of Berwyn bank.
Midcheshireman

B1 MAYFLOWER and D49 MORAYSHIRE, both supposedly in LNER apple green livery, but very different when seen together - which is correct?

Midcheshireman

The same combination is seen near Berwyn on 19th April 2009.

Dave Collier

The railway used to run a Sunday dining train called the *Mid-Day Belle*, it comprised a set of pullman cars and a converted horsebox as a power generator. Sadly the train no longer runs. Here it is crossing the Dee Bridge behind 60103 FLYING SCOTSMAN.

Midcheshireman

Gresley A4 Pacific 60009 UNION OF SOUTH AFRICA waits at Llangollen Goods Junction in this 1990s view.

Midcheshireman

Ex LNER observation coach E1719 is on the rear of a train at Llangollen on 17th April 2009.

Dave Collier

This is the unique ex LNER Thompson buffet car which once saw servie on the Eastern Region's *Elizabethan* express - mogul 5322 steams on into the distance.

Midcheshireman

Newly built A1 Pacific 60163 TORNADO enters Glyndyfrdwy during the somewhat damp *Steel, Steam and Stars III* event.

Leslie Platt

Built in 1898, Metropolitan Railway No 1 was a guest at the 2008 Autumn Gala. Here she is drifting down hill along the river towards Glyndwfrdwy.

Midcheshireman

British Railways 76079 near Glyndyfrdwy in June 1996.

Dave Collier

78019 leaves Llangollen during the first *Steel, Steam and Stars* Gala in 2007.

Midcheshireman

80072 arriving into Carrog on 9th June 2018.

Jeff Albiston

80072 departing from Glyndyfrdwy, and carrying a *North Wales Radio Land Cruise* headboard during the *Along Cambrian Lines* Steam Gala on 10th April 2016.

Jeff Albiston

80072 in weathered condition at Ty Newydd with the Suburban coaches during the 1960s weekend on 26th July 2014.

Jeff Albiston

Having obtained a clear road visiting British Railways standard tank 80136 awaits the guard's whistle to depart Glyndyfrdwy for Carrog.
Midcheshireman

92203 BLACK PRINCE emerges from the fog with a *Santa Special* during the 1990s.
Midcheshireman

Looking smart in BR lined green livery 92214 CENTRAL STAR is seen heading towards the lens with a passenger service for Carrog at Fisherman's Crossing during *Steel, Steam and Stars IV* on the 7th of March 2015.

Martyn Tattam

On the opening day of *Steam, Steel and Stars* 2015, two of the visiting locos pull away from Berwyn with the late running 11.23 Llangollen - Corwen. Leading is 9F 2-10-0 92214 CENTRAL STAR, with Bulleid Pacific 34092 CITY OF WELLS as train engine.

Midcheshireman

9F 92214 CENTRAL STAR sits in Glyndyfrdwy station with the firedoor open painting the smoke above it the colour of flame with a late return train to Llangollen, during *Steel, Steam and Stars IV* on 13th March 2015.

Lawrie Rose

American built USA 2-8-0 5197 rolls into Glyndyfrdwy station with a demonstration freight during a Wartime Weekend in the early 2000s.
Midcheshireman

'Austerity' 0-6-0ST WELSH GUARDSMAN, formerly WD 71516, is pictured on a test run following overhaul at Llangollen, prior to its return to its home base at the Gwili Railway.

Leslie Platt

The *Back To the 90s* event on the 7th March 2020 featured the railway's first engine AUSTIN No. 1 ran at the railway for the first time this millennium.

Douglas Hebson

The same locomotive is seen crossing the Dee Bridge in the 1980s, in its No. 5459 alter ego. It also carried the name BURTONWOOD BREWER at various times.

Midcheshireman

This classic 1953 Hunslet 0-6-ST from Darfield Colliery near Barnsley was resident at Llangollen for many years but is now back in Yorkshire at the Embsay & Bolton Abbey Railway. Here it is taking it relatively easy on banking duties near the Dee Bridge.

Midcheshireman

DARFIELD No. 1 arriving at Glyndyfrdwy with the 1440 from Llangollen on 7th August 1992.

Phil Barnes

Resident Hudswell Clarke 1731 JENNIFER is seen at Garth y Dwr on a Carrog bound covid service on 27th August 2020.

Kenny Felstead

In the spring and autumn the railway gives its smaller engines an occasional outing. This is JESSIE, built by Hunslet in 1937, a former steelworks shunter from Cardiff with a whistle tone significantly deeper than a Stanier hooter! It is seen passing Garth y Dwr.

Midcheshireman

THOMAS and PERCY entertain the crowds at Llangollen during a *Thomas* event on 9th August 2007.

Phil Barnes

Standing in for the more usual locomotive, Hunslet 0-6-0ST JESSIE, temporarily rebuilt as a side tank and painted blue to act as *Thomas* in future themed events lifts the noon Carrog - Llangollen local away from Glyndyfrdwy.

Midcheshireman

Llangollen yard shunter, 0-4-0 PILKINGTON, is pictured at rest in 2016.

Andrew Budd

One of the first rail locomotives to venture up the line after lockdown, escorting the weeding vehicle, was Class 08 13265, pictured at Carrog on 6th July 2020.

Douglas Hebson

With a prototypical ballast working visiting Class 25 D7535 from the South Devon Railway is seen heading around the curve at Garth y Dwr during the *Foxcote Manor Returns* Gala on the 13th of October 2019.

Martyn Tattam

Class 26 D5310 makes a night time departure from Glyndyfrdwy on 4th January 2014.

Leslie Platt

Class 31 5580 enters the loop at Glyndyfrdwy on 26th August 2012.

Leslie Platt

The 10am Llangollen - Corwen leaves Berwyn, not behind the expected Great Western prairie, but instead behind Class 37 6940.

Midcheshireman

Class 37 6940 at Garth y Dwr on 9th June 2018.

Jeff Albiston

Following a series of track-side fires during the heatwave steam locos were withdrawn from the Llangollen Railway and diesel locomotives took their place. Class 37 D6940 is seen leaving Glyndyfrdwy heading for Llangollen on 26th June 2018.

Leslie Platt

Brush built Class 47 47449 in the shed yard at Llangollen on 28th April 2001.

Phil Barnes

The same locomotive, now renumbered 1566, arriving into Glyndyfrdwy on a wet day during the *Western Changeover* Gala on 13th April 2018.

Jeff Albiston

Crewe-built 1566 running round at Carrog on 22nd April 2018.

Leslie Platt

A scene from one of the railway's winter warmer events - a Class 104 DMU for Llangollen waits in the platform at Carrog as class 5 4-6-0 45337 enters the station with a Llangollen - Corwen stopper, GWR 2-8-0 3802 can also be glimpsed by the signalbox.

Midcheshireman

The 15:00 departure from Llangollen heads towards Corwen after calling at Carrog on 27th March 2015.

Leslie Platt

The only survivior of the distinctive art deco style Wickham built Class 109 diesel multiple units leaves Llangollen with the 10.30 to Carrog.

Midcheshireman

A Carrog bound train hauled by D5310 arrives at Glyndyfrdwy, passing the Class 109 DMU in the other platform, on 30th July 2011.

Leslie Platt

The Class 109 DMU is framed by lineside equipment as it leaves Glyndyfrdwy on 11th October 2010.

Leslie Platt

A technical fault caused the Class 121 "Bubble Car" to spend a few extra minutes in the up passing loop at Deeside on 20th June 2015. The single-car dmu was visiting the railway as part of a DMU Gala.

Leslie Platt

A Polish tank locomotive is seen on 28th April 2001 in the large workshop facility at Llangollen, being restored for operation on another UK heritage railway.

Phil Barnes

7822 FOXCOTE MANOR drifts into Llangollen station on 10th September 2020.

Mark Faulkner

Preservation is about more than trains, there is the equipment too, such as this vintage token machine inside the signalbox at Glyndyfrdwy in 2011.

Leslie Platt

Authentically attired passengers visit on 14 April 2019 when the railway staged a 1940s weekend.

Leslie Platt

Sunset at Glyndyfrdwy on 29th September 2012.

Leslie Platt

Double rainbows are a sign of good luck aren't they? Carrog on 5th November 2017.

Douglas Hebson

The RRV making its way down the Corwen site, now with completed track layout. 28th December 2019.

Douglas Hebson

Corwen starting to come together, still a long way to go, but one step closer to seeing a train arrive. 26th September 2020.

Douglas Hebson

A view of the Corwen site from above, with a lovely view from the signal box. 28th November 2020.

Douglas Hebson

This is the view on 28th April 2001 of the start of work on the extension from Carrog to Corwen, taken from the road overbridge adjacent to Carrog station.

Phil Barnes

The closing event of the 9-day *Steel, Steam & Stars II* Gala organised by the 6880 Betton Grange Society, held at the Llangollen Railway in April 2009. The cavalcade of ten locomotives is seen approaching Carrog on 26th April 2009.

Leslie Platt